I0491741

BROWSER VS BUYER

Optimize Your Ecommerce Website & Get More Sales!

Elise Nelson

Copyright © 2020 Elise Nelson

All rights reserved

The characters and events portrayed in this book are fictitious.
Any similarity to real persons, living or dead, is coincidental
and not intended by the author.

No part of this book may be reproduced, or stored in a retrieval
system, or transmitted in any form or by any means, electronic,
mechanical, photocopying, recording, or otherwise, without
express written permission of the publisher.

ISBN: 979670961318

Cover design by: Elise Nelson
Printed in the United States of America

Dedicated to all the small business owners who have trusted me with their businesses.

CONTENTS

PREFACE

Ring. Ring. Ring.

You pick-up your cell phone and it's a number you don't recognize. You decide you'll risk it and answer the phone.

You're greeted by someone who mispronounces your name and can barely speak English. They immediately ask you for your social security number. You laugh and tell them to remove you from their call list.

After hanging up the phone you think to yourself, "Who could be that stupid?".

But the truth is, it's all about numbers...

No matter how bad the pitch, no matter how awful the experience, some people will fall for anything.

This is true for your website as well.

No matter how many warning signs you have on your website & no matter how poorly it is designed, if you send enough traffic to it, eventually someone will buy.

But, is that REALLY what you want? Do you want your website to be like the telemarketer of ecommerce shops?

Do you want your website to create an experience of mistrust and concern for your shoppers? OR do you want to invoke a feeling of trust & excitement?

Do you want to anticipate your shopper's questions, provide them with answers, and make shopping your website simple? Or do you want to rely on sending as many people as possible to your website knowing that eventually you'll get sales.

To be clear, there is no wrong answer here.

There is nothing "wrong" with taking the "more traffic equals more sales" route.

In fact I HIGHLY recommend that you send as much traffic as possible to your website, when it's ready.

But if ALL you are relying on is more traffic, you might be missing out on creating the BEST experience for your shoppers. Plus, you'll ultimately invest more (money and/or time) in getting those sales than is necessary.

Think about it...if 1 out of 100 people buy and you want 1 sale you have to get 100 people to your site.

On the other hand, if 1 out of 50 people buy, you only need to get 50 people to your site to get that 1 sale.

This book is all about increasing the percentage of people who purchase when they visit your website.

Therefore, this book is for you if you are ready to invest a little time and/or money right now to improve your purchase conversion so that you can spend less money and/or time in sending traffic to your website for the life of your business.

This book is NOT for you if you don't want to improve the shopping experience on your website and would rather spend money and/or time in sending as much traffic as possible to get sales.

CH 1 - SHOPPER MINDSET

Buyers, Browsers, & Purchasers

Susie Q is your perfect Shopper, your "ideal" client. If you were targeting your perfect audience she would be #1 on your list.

Susie Q learns about your product & visits your website because she's curious about what you have to offer. She has no intention of buying anything.

By the time she looks at 3 pages on your website she's still not convinced to make a purchase, so she leaves.

What happened?

Is the reason she didn't make a purchase because she started her visit knowing that she wouldn't? OR is it because YOU didn't address her needs?

It could be either reason. But if you don't have a website set-up to walk a customer down the path to purchase, it's probably at least partially your fault.

Before we dive into this, I want to introduce you to

another customer.

Your products are perfect for Jane Doe. You're like peanut butter and jelly or chips and salsa. It's a match made in heaven.

Jane Doe sees one of your products and knows it's something she just has to have. She is ready to pay before she even gets to your website.

She looks at the product page, adds it to her cart, and completes checkout. She's incredibly excited & can't wait for her new purchase to arrive.

Why was it so easy to make the sale to Jane Doe?

Is it because she intended to make a purchase? OR is it because you addressed her needs?

In this chapter we're going to be talking about the "Shopper Mindset", how it impacts your ability to make a sale, and why you should use it as the basis for your website layout.

Shoppers

Everyone who visits your website is a "Shopper". They are on your website to find something.

If you've been in ecommerce for any amount of time you know that MOST of your Shoppers will not make a purchase.

The average in ecommerce is a 1-2% purchase conversion rate. This means that only 1-2% of Shoppers who visit your site will actually make a purchase.

In other words, if you have an average website, you will need to send 50 to 100 people to your site to get just ONE sale.

But, in my experience, MANY ecommerce sites are not average. MANY ecommerce sites have a lower than average conversion rate. It might take 150, 200, or even 300 web visitors before your site gets a single sale.

Does that mean you should just throw in the towel and give up? No.

It means you need to think about what you can do to improve your purchase conversion rate so that it takes less Shoppers to get one sale. THEN, you start sending more traffic and generating more and more sales.

To improve your purchase conversion rate you need

to think about who your Shoppers are and why they are on your site.

Buyers Vs Browsers

Who are your Shoppers and what do they want?

EVERY Shopper who comes to your site falls into one of two categories. They are either a "Buyer" or a "Browser".

Buyers come to your site with the intention of making a purchase. They might have seen a specific product on social media or through advertisement or they could already be acquainted with your brand.

Regardless of why they come to your website, Buyers are there to make a purchase.

Browsers, on the other hand, are NOT on your site to make a purchase.

Browsers come to your site because they are curious and want to see what you have to offer.

Browsers do NOT intend to make a purchase.

Who do you think it is easier to convince to make a purchase? Browsers or Buyers?

Buyers.

Does that mean you cannot convince Browsers to make a purchase? NO!

Browsers will also purchase IF you address their needs.

The problem is that most ecommerce shops do NOT address Browsers' needs.

Most ecommerce shops focus on the easy sale and ONLY address Buyers' needs.

The funny thing is that Buyers will purchase even when your site has a less than the ideal user experience, so it really takes VERY minimal effort to get them to purchase once you get them to your website.

Plus, most ecommerce owners consider ANY sale to be a "win". So if they're making ANY sales it feels like they are doing a "great job", so they never take the extra step to reach Browsers.

But, with just a little understanding you can increase how much your Buyers spend when they make a purchase. AND when you address Browser's needs, you can convince them to make a purchase also.

Are you starting to get excited?

In just a few chapters we're going to be discussing how to increase the number of sales on your website AND how to increase how much is spent on each sale.

Both of these things can make a HUGE impact on how much money you make. After all, if you're really honest you are in business to make sales and support your family. It's just an amazing bonus that you get to help your customers along the way.

Buyers

Do you remember Jane Doe from the beginning of this chapter? She came to your website to make a purchase and she did make a purchase.

Jane Doe is a Buyer.

Buyers make up a VERY small amount of the Shoppers on your website.

But, Buyers are EASY to convince to make a purchase because it is what they want.

In a later chapter we'll talk about how to get Buyers to purchase MORE products and raise your average order value (AOV) to increase your sales. But right now, let's talk about your Buyers' needs and make sure your website is addressing them.

Buyers come to your site to buy. This means you need to make it easy for them to find what they want. If you don't, even Buyers won't make a purchase.

You NEED to have your website broken down into easy to shop categories because Buyers shop "narrow". They are "targeted" Shoppers. They want to find what they want quickly.

Narrow categories are "friends" to Buyers.

So, what do Buyers want? They want an easy to shop websites with intuitive categories.

Browsers

Now let's talk about Susie Q. Susie Q was curious about your website. She did not intend to make a purchase when she visited your website, and low and behold she didn't.

Susie Q is a Browser.

Browsers make up a VERY large number of the Shoppers who visit your website.

Browsers are HARDER to convince to make a purchase, but there are so many more of them it's still worth it to address their needs on your website.

Browsers come to your website out of curiosity. They want to see EVERYTHING you have to offer.

Browsers do NOT want to make any decisions because they don't know what they want. They want you to give them a summary of what you offer on a silver platter.

Browsers are equivalent to "Window Shoppers".

Have you ever been a "Window Shopper"? You visit a store just to "look around" with no intention of actually making a purchase. Maybe you are tagging along with a friend while they shop.

Do you sometimes make a purchase even though you were only "Window Shopping"? I'm sure you have.

This is because Browsers CAN be convinced to purchase IF you show them something they want *(even if they never intended to make a purchase from the start)*.

Browsers shop "broad". They are "Window Shoppers". They want to have everything given to them on a silver platter. They will NOT search for things.

Narrow categories are the "enemy" of Browsers.

So, what do Browsers want? They want a way to look at everything without making any decisions.

Purchasers

Before we move on to the next section, I want to introduce you to one more Shopper. This Shopper is what I call a "Purchaser".

Purchasers are Shoppers who actually make a purchase on your website.

Purchasers can start out as Buyers or as Browsers.

NO ONE comes to your site as a Purchaser.

YOU are responsible for converting your Buyers & Browsers into Purchasers.

The "buck stops with you", so to speak.

So, stop thinking you have NO control. Stop thinking it's ALL luck or ALL out of your hands.

You do have SOME control.

Take responsibility and let's get your website setup with the best shopping experience you can offer to convert those Buyers & Browsers into Purchasers!

CH 2 - PSYCHIC MENUS

Answering Shopper's Questions Before They Ask

W hat does it mean to be psychic? A psychic is typically considered to be able to tell the future or read minds or some other form of gaining knowledge outside the normal course of knowledge acquisition.

I've never been to a psychic. But, I've seen them on movies & tv.

I've never had a desire to be a psychic. But, this chapter is all about making your website "psychic".

I want to teach you how to create "Psychic Menus" so that your Shoppers can get instant answers to their questions.

Because online if you don't provide instant answers *(almost like you are psychic & know what your shoppers are thinking)* you will lose your audience.

This chapter is ALL about your Menus.

Your Menus are seen by EVERY Shopper on your website because they are on EVERY page. This means your Menus are INCREDIBLY important.

We are going to spend a LOT of time on your Menus

before we even look at your product pages, because your Menus are INCREDIBLY important.

Do I need to say that again? Your Menus are INCREDIBLY important!

◆ ◆ ◆

Header & Footer

The goal of your Menus is to overcome objections and to move the Shopper down the path to a purchase. Therefore, your Menu needs to answer EVERY question your Shopper has.

There should be 2 Menus on every ecommerce site. These Menus are your Header & your Footer.

The Header Menu is positioned at the top of every page of your website. The goal of the Header Menu is to direct the customer to where you want them to go AND to answer FAQ *(Frequently Asked Questions)* without causing "Analysis Paralysis" *(the inability to make a decision because there are too many options)* AND to promote brand recognition.

The Footer Menu is positioned at the bottom of every page of your website. The goal of your Footer

Menu is to answer FAQ AND promote brand recognition AND provide social media links AND provide necessary website information.

Header Structure

The very first thing to consider about your Header is how "tall" it is.

Your Header should take up no more than ¼ of a page "above the fold" *(the part of the page that is visible without scrolling).* This means ¾ of the page is available for other content WITHOUT scrolling & not used for your Header Menu.

This is important because most Shoppers will not scroll through your entire page. Therefore, it's important to make sure EVERY page gives them as much info as possible, as quickly as possible, without scrolling *(whenever possible).*

The next thing to consider is how many "things" there are in your Header. This should absolutely NEVER exceed 7-8 "things".

ANYTHING that is in your Header is considered in this count. Possibilities include your logo, a site-wide notice, menu items, search, shopping cart, social media links, phone number, address, etc.

Having too many "things" in the Header Menu can cause "Analysis Paralysis" *(the inability to make a decision because there are too many options)* which will stop your Shoppers on their path to purchase and decrease your purchase conversion *(and ultimately your sales)*.

◆ ◆ ◆

Header Content

If you could only pick ONE reason why you have an ecommerce shop you would have to admit that the reason is to make money.

That's not to say that there aren't 100 actual reasons. You may want to help your audience, you may be donating to charity, you may legitimately just love what you do, you might just believe in the "cause".

But, the reality is...the honest truth is...that you are in this to make money.

Your website needs to reflect that goal.

The NUMBER ONE GOAL of your website is to get people to make a purchase.

In order to get them to make a purchase you have to tell them what to do next to move them down the path to purchase. You also need to answer their questions & overcome objections.

THIS is the purpose of the Header. It is to KEEP THEM on your website until you make a sale. Period.

Anything that distracts from this purpose does NOT belong in your Header. Anything that takes them away from your website does NOT belong in your Header.

This means social media links, phone numbers, etc do NOT belong in your Header. *(NOTE: this advice is assuming that your number one goal is to sell online. IF you have a large offline presence there MIGHT be reasons to alter this...BUT, for the most part I recommend following this rule 100% of the time)*

Now that you know what not to put in your Header Menu, what should be in your Header Menu?

Do you remember what I said the goal of the Header Menu was at the beginning of this chapter? "The goal of the Header Menu is to direct the customer to where you want them to go AND to answer FAQ without causing Analysis Paralysis AND to promote brand recognition."

Here's an example of a Header:

❖ ❖ ❖

Logo

One thing that pretty much every website I've ever reviewed has in common is that they all had a logo in the Header. *(If you'd like more information about having me review your website please visit: www.My-ScheduledBiz.com/Easy)*

PHOTO COURTESY OF: GATHERED-SOWN.COM

This is one thing that hopefully you got right also.

The reason it's important to have your logo in the Header is because it promotes brand recognition.

While the ultimate purpose of the website IS to

promote Shoppers to make a purchase, not every Shopper will purchase the first time they visit your website.

This means you need to be sure that *(at a minimum)* they recognize your brand the next time they see it.

Familiarity often turns into trust with time. Building that familiarity *(and ultimately trust)* will hopefully make them more likely to make a purchase in the future.

So, if you can't make a sale with a Shopper you need to at least get them to recognize your brand for your next attempt at getting the sale. That is why you NEED to have a recognizable logo in your Header Menu.

Shop

The next "thing" in your Header Menu is the "Shop" button.

It is ESSENTIAL that the Shop Menu is obvious and stands out from everything else in your header. So, try to make it different in some way. You can use a different color, add a button that says "Shop Now", add an underline to the Shop Menu item. Do whatever you can do to make shopping the obvious next step for your customer.

PHOTO COURTESY OF: MACHLAO.COM

This Shop button/menu item *(or even one of each as shown in the example Header above)* is your Call To Action *(CTA)*. This is what you are telling them to do. It "calls them" to do something. In this case, it "calls them" to SHOP.

When you hover over *(place your mouse over)* this Menu it should open up to show a series of additional menu items. When you click on this Menu/button it should take them to a page with ALL your products on it.

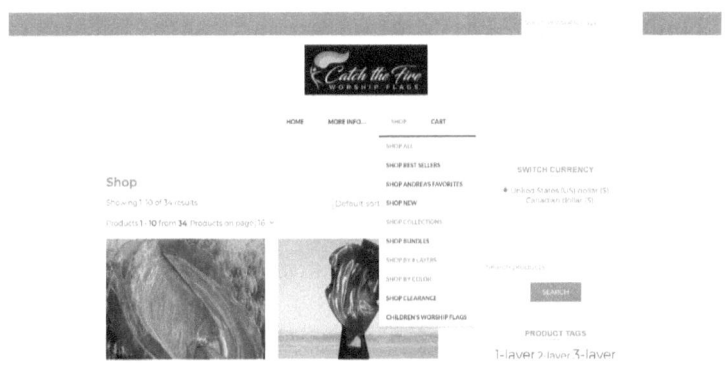

PHOTO COURTESY OF: CATCHTHEFIREWORSHIPFLAGS.COM

The VERY FIRST menu item in the Shop Menu should be "Shop All" or "All Products". It is important it says "ALL".

This menu item is specifically for your Browsers so that they can see EVERYTHING you offer. The "Shop All" menu item should take them to a page with ALL your products on it. *(NOTE: Be sure that these products are in a random order so that your Shoppers can see a sampling of your various products all on the first page.)*

The NEXT menu item in the Shop Menu should be "Best Sellers". This menu item is also for your Browsers because it is a way to show them a sample of your products without them having to make any actual decisions about what they want.

The THIRD menu item in the Shop Menu should be "New Arrivals". This menu item is for your Browsers because they won't have to make any decisions, but it is also for your Buyers because they can easily see the newest products and possibly add one of them to their purchase easily.

Once you have these three menu items in your Shop Menu, it is finally time to address your categories.

Categories are specifically to help your Buyers find what they want to purchase.

We'll break these down in the next section.

For now, let's move on to the last few menu items in your Shop Menu.

After your Shop Categories, the next menu item should be "Gift Cards" *(if you offer Gift Cards)*.

Then "Sale" and/or "Clearance" menu items.

If you offer wholesale or have a list of stores who sell your products you could add menu items for those in the Shop Menu as well.

That sums up your Shop Menu. Now on to discussing your Shop Categories.

Shop Categories

Most ecommerce shops seem to have at least some level of understanding with this part of the Shop Menu. But, they have a tendency to miss out on some of the options.

It is essential that you think about your product and decide how you can sort it in several different ways so that your shoppers can find what they want easily.

First, consider what "Product Types" you offer. If you sell jewelry, this is bracelets, necklaces, rings, etc. If you sell clothing, this is tops, pants, dresses, etc.

Second, consider what "Product Sizes" you offer. If you sell jewelry, this is probably not a good way to sort your product. But if you sell clothing, breaking shopping down by size is probably an ESSENTIAL way to give your Shoppers so that they don't become discouraged by finding things they want to buy that aren't available in their size.

Third, consider what "Product Colors" you offer. If you sell jewelry, this may be a way of breaking down your product by metal type. For example, I never wear gold-tone jewelry, so being able to just shop pieces that are silver-tone is incredibly useful if I'm shopping for jewelry. If you sell clothing, this same rule applies. It also makes it significantly easier to shop for specific events *(think Valentine's Day or Patrick's Day)*.

Fourth, consider if there's some other way of sorting that makes sense for your products. If you sell jewelry, you may want to consider sorting by metal due to allergies. If you sell paintings you may separate landscapes from stills or portraits.

The number of ways you can sort your products will determine whether you have one Menu level or if you need to use sub-Menus.

For example, your Shop Menu may have the following menu items (~):
~ Shop All
~ Best Sellers
~ New Arrivals
~ Kitchen
~ Bedroom
~ Bathroom
~ Gift Cards
~ Clearance

Or your Shop Menu may have the following menu items (~) with sub-menu items (-):
~ Shop All
~ Best Sellers
~ New Arrivals
~ Shop by Type
　　- Tops
　　- Pants
　　- Dresses
~ Shop by Color
　　- Red

- Orange
- Yellow
- Green
- Black
~ Shop by Size
- Women's
- Plus Size
- Teen
~ Gift Cards
~ Clearance

Whichever way you decide to organize your categories, keep in mind that the goal of this section of your Shop Menu is to provide your Buyers with a direct path to purchase. You do NOT want to under-categorize, thereby making it too difficult for them to find what they want.

◆ ◆ ◆

The "Other" Menu

The next "thing" in your Header Menu is the "Other" Menu...this can be called "More", "More Info", "Information", "About" or pretty much anything you can think of that portrays the idea that this Menu is NOT about shopping....it is everything else.

The first menu item you should put in your Other Menu is your blog *(if you have one)* because this is a way to introduce your Shoppers to your brand and hopefully bring them back to your site over and over again.

The next menu item should be your "About" page. It is essential that this page is easy to read. Therefore be sure to use text formatting *(bold, italic, underlines)* AND Titles between sections to facilitate quick reading and comprehension. Your About Page should provide a story about why you do what you do, why it is important, and who it impacts *(think about your customers or your cause or a charity if you support one with your business)*. You should also have Social Media Links on your About Page.

The third menu item in your Other Menu should be "Contact". Your contact page should include your email address, phone, & address *(if you have a physical location)*, a field to input any questions, and possibly even a link to your Facebook Chat/Customer Service Chat. You should also include Social Media Links on this page.

Next you should have a menu item for "Reviews".

This link should take your Shoppers to a page FULL of reviews. This will build confidence in your site and help take you out of the "telemarketer" space in your Shopper's minds. This page can single-handedly help your website appear more legitimate and less-likely to be a "rip off". It is INCREDIBLY important to work towards trust and separate yourself from the scam sites that permeate the internet. Don't skip this menu item.

After your Reviews menu item you should have a "FAQ" (Frequently Asked Questions) menu item, a "Shipping" menu item, & a "Returns" menu item. These 3 menu items can lead to separate pages on your website OR all three can lead to the same page on your website. Regardless, you still need all 3 menu items in your Other Menu because when a Shopper is looking for a specific answer these three menu items are most likely EXACTLY what they are looking for, so make it easy for them to find what they want. The content on these pages is going to vary based upon the product you are selling, but just like the About Page having good text formatting and headers *(so that your Shopper can find answers to their questions as quickly as possible)* is essential.

The final menu item in your Other Menu should be "My Account" or "Sign In" or "Register". In other words, a way for them to access their order history *(if they have one)*. If you do not have your Shoppers set-up an account you can skip this menu item.

There you have it! You have completed your "Other" Menu!

Even More

After you have a Logo, a Shop Menu, a Shop Button *(if possible)*, and an Other Menu there are 2 more "things" you need to include on your Header Menu.

First, you need to be sure to have a place to search OR a link to a page where your customer can search for what they want. This is important to your Buyers because it makes it so they can look for EXACTLY what brought them to your website and move them directly into a purchase.

Second, you need to have a link to your Shopping Cart, so that it is easy for your Shoppers to get to checkout and make their purchase.

Once you have completed these final two "things" your Header Menu is complete! Congratulations!

Next, we'll be talking about your Footer Menu.

Footer Structure

Your Footer needs to stand out from the rest of your website, so that it is obvious that your Shoppers have come to another menu. Therefore, make sure your Footer is a different color than the rest of your webpage. This is not to say that you don't use the color anywhere else. This just means it is a different color from the rest of the website's background color.

Just like your Header Menu your Footer Menu should be succinct. Since it is at the bottom of every page the height is not as important, but it should definitely NEVER exceed one page. You should not have to scroll to see your entire Footer.

It is also essential that you organize all the Footer information in such a way that it is easy for your Shoppers to find what they are looking for. So, be sure to use Titles to separate similar information.

Footer Content

Do you remember what I said the goal of the Footer is at the beginning of this chapter? "The goal of your Footer Menu is to answer FAQ AND promote brand recognition AND provide social media links AND provide necessary website information."

If you're paying attention you'll notice that the first 2 in this list are the same as the goal of the Header Menu. That is why everything we just discussed for your Header Menu should also go in your Footer Menu *(including your Logo)*.

The only exception is if you are using sub-menus in your Header. If you are sorting your categories down into 2 or more categories you will not list all of the sub-menus in your footer, only the main menus.

This is the example from the Header Menu:
~ Shop All
~ Best Sellers
~ New Arrivals
~ Shop by Type
   - Tops
   - Pants

- Dresses
~ Shop by Color
   - Red
   - Orange
   - Yellow
   - Green
   - Black
~ Shop by Size
   - Women's
   - Plus Size
   - Teen
~ Gift Cards
~ Clearance

In the Footer this would look like this instead:
~ Shop All
~ Best Sellers
~ New Arrivals
~ Shop by Product Type
~ Shop by Color
~ Shop by Size
~ Gift Cards
~ Clearance

When your Shopper clicks on "Shop by _____" it will need to take them to a page that lets them choose which sort they want to use. This means you need to have a page on your website that breaks down each sort type.

In this example you would have a "Shop by Product

Type", "Shop by Color", & "Shop by Size" page for your website.

On each of these pages you would have images/links to click to take them to each sub-menu item *(red, blue, green, etc)*. If you can add filters to your shop offering these sub-menus as filter options, be sure to set that up as well.

Your Footer Menu should also include links to your social media to promote engagement with your brand which can help build trust and recognition.

A few bonuses you may want to include in your Footer Menu include a Chat Widget *(Facebook Messenger allows you to set this up for free)* and an email list opt-in. We'll discuss incentives for opting in to your email list in a future chapter. But, for now, I just wanted to mention that the Footer is a good place to put these website features.

Finally, your Footer Menu is the place to put the more "boring" aspects of your website, like Copyright, Privacy Policy, and Terms of Website Use.

Here are a few Footer Menu examples for you to draw inspiration from:

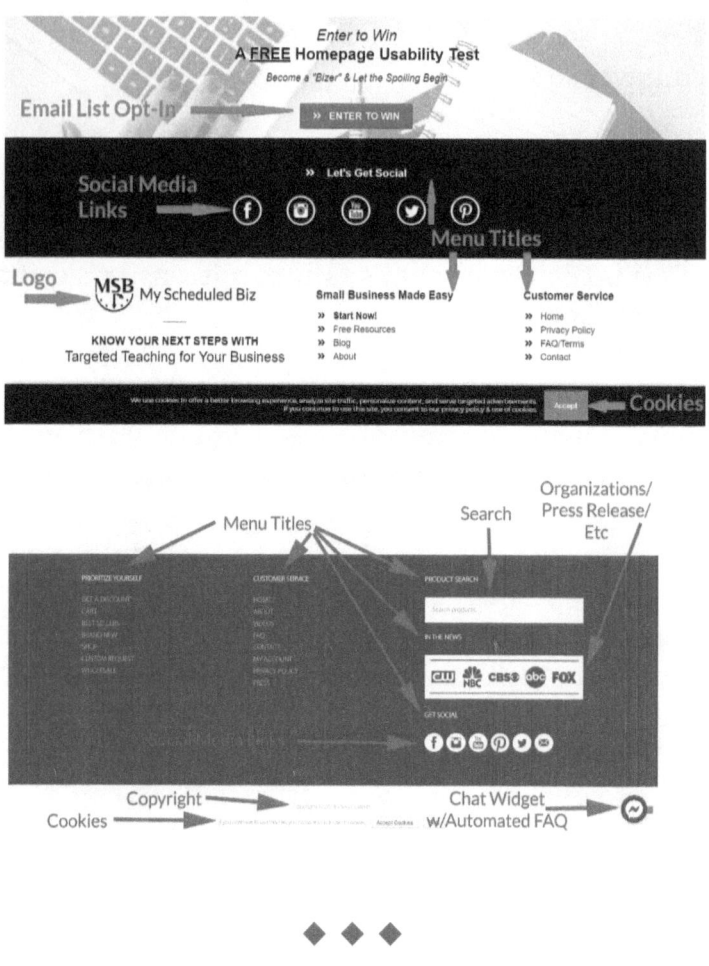

❖ ❖ ❖

Now It's Your Turn

Now that you understand (hopefully) the purpose of your Header & Footer Menus, what belongs in each, and why...It's time to optimize your website.

Before you move on to the next chapter, go make these changes on your website OR write an email explaining the changes to your website manager.

It is ESSENTIAL that your menus are laid out so that your Shoppers can find what they want before you move on.

In the next chapter we're going to be discussing your Shop Pages.

CH 3 - SHOP PAGES

Consistency Is The Key

You are looking for the perfect gift for your best friend's birthday. She LOVES "shopping small" to support local small business owners, so you decide to visit a few local shops instead of the big retailers at the mall.

You find two stores that are close to each other that sound like they may have what you need.

You enter the first store and are shocked at how dimly lit it is. There's also some strange smell permeating the building.

You go to the aisle that is supposed to have what you're looking for, but the boxes are all shoved at weird angles. Plus, many of the products that aren't boxed are flung on the shelves haphazardly or pushed to the back so you can barely even see them. Half the products do not have price tags.

It's seriously the most disorganized store you have ever visited. You wouldn't be surprised if no one had ever straightened the shelves the entire time it's been opened.

Plus, the employees are all yelling at each other about something & making a terrible racket.

It's difficult to focus on what's actually available because it is such a disaster. You stare at the shelves for a few minutes, snap a picture *(because it seems so unreal)* and walk out of the store.

Back in the car, you are incredibly grateful there's a second store, and make the 2 minute drive, hoping this one will be a better shopping experience.

You arrive at the second store, walk in the door and an awesome song is playing. The store is well-lit and the air smells fresh. You immediately feel more comfortable.

You walk to the appropriate aisle, which is clearly organized and everything has an easily readable price tag. Within a few minutes you find the perfect gift for your friend.

You head to the cashier *(stopping to pick up a pack of gum on the way)*, chat for a few minutes, and make your purchase.

Which type of shopping experience do you want for your website Shoppers?

I truly hope you picked the second store...if you didn't, I'm worried for you.

I understand that you cannot control smell and

having music playing on your website will actually probably be considered annoying rather than a positive *(the way it was in the above example)*, but this idea still applies to your website.

You HAVE TO provide a good user experience to put your Shoppers at ease enough to make a purchase.

Your job is to make your ecommerce shop appear "put together". To make it seem like you "know what you are doing". Even if you don't. This builds your Shoppers' confidence in your store so that they feel comfortable making a purchase.

How do you accomplish this on your website? There are quite a few ways and we'll cover many of them. But the purpose of this chapter is to discuss the actual Shop Pages *(not the Product Pages)*. So, that's where we're going to start.

The BIGGEST way to turn people off on your Shop Pages *(the pages that show many of your products so that Shoppers can choose which products to actually look at)* can be your photos.

It's important that your Shop Pages are like the organized, easy to browse shelves in the second store *(not the crazy shelves in the first store)*. You do this by having photos that are intentional, not haphazard.

Photo Ratio

The very first thing you need is photos that are ALL formatted to the same ratio. Most of the time I recommend a 1:1 ratio because this is the easiest to accomplish. It's a square.

As long as you take *(or edit)* your photos into a square, all your photos *(on your Shop & Product Pages)* will look uniform & intentional. This also has the distinct advantage of being good for social media as well.

However, there are a few products that lend themselves better to other ratios. For example, clothing is typically a 2:3 or 3:4 ratio *(resulting in a vertical rectangle)*.

The point here is to choose what ratio you plan to use and then make EVERY photo of your products in this ratio. This will help your products look spaced evenly on the "shelves"of your Shop Pages.

Photo Type

The next thing you need to consider is what types of photos you want to use. There are two options. Option 1 is white background product photos. The second option is lifestyle photos.

White Background Product Photo

The only thing in a white background product photo is the product. These photos are used to let your products "speak for themselves".

The most important aspect of a white background product photo is that the color of the background has to be the same in EVERY photo so that the photo looks intentional.

If the white changes from photo to photo it gives the impression that the photos are being thrown together by someone who does not know what they are doing.

If you don't know what you are doing & cannot achieve a cohesive look with the SAME background color in all images, then you should consider hiring someone to do the photo editing for you.

One of the first questions I get is, "Does it have to be a WHITE background?" The short answer is, "Yes! It has to be a WHITE background". However, there are SOME exceptions. But, most likely, your shop is NOT one of them.

To be clear, the point of a white background product photo is to let the product shine by placing it on a neutral, consistent background. However, what is considered neutral may vary for your product. Neutrals for baby products may be white, yellow, pink, and blue. Technically you can use any of these colors *(or a combination of them)* as the background colors in your photos as long as they are edited in such a manner that the colors are consistent.

Most people do not have the technical skills necessary to pull these alternate background colors off though. So, I suggest following the letter of the rule and sticking with white.

Having poorly edited photos is one of the easiest ways to delegitimize your website & ruin all of your hard work. So, don't risk these unless you are 100% certain you can edit your photos properly.

Lifestyle Photos

Lifestyle photos contain your product and other items/people, but the product is the focus. When looking at the photo it should be obvious what item the photo is about.

Lifestyle photos are used to show your product in use and/or tell a story so that your Shopper can imagine the product in their life.

The key to lifestyle photos is to use a consistent "look". The easiest way to do this is to always use the same photo filter on your images.

It is also incredibly important that these photos are not over cluttered. Less is more when it comes to lifestyle photos.

◆ ◆ ◆

Photo Consistency

The easiest way to make your Shop Pages look uniform is to choose ONE of these types of photos to use on your shop pages (*you'll still need both types for your product pages though*).

But, you can use both types as long as it looks intentional. You can make it look intentional by being random in which products receive white-background versus lifestyle photos OR by setting up your shop with an intentional pattern.

Possible patterns may include alternating white background & lifestyle product photos or alternating white background & lifestyle rows/columns.

Regardless of which photos you choose to use and how you choose to organize them, it's important that your method is consistent throughout your ENTIRE shop.

When it comes to your Shop Pages, consistency is the key to providing a pleasant user experience for your customers. Don't be like store number 1. Be like the second store. Invite your customers in, put them at ease, and start making more sales.

CH 4 - PRODUCT PAGES

Be The Sales Associate

I t has happened. Your computer has crashed and it cannot be recovered.

You find yourself at the computer store face to face with the sales associate explaining what you need.

They show you a computer, but it is not what you want. You tell them it's not a good fit.

They say, "Well...Thanks so much, have a great day" and walk away.

Is that good customer service? Does that make you want to buy a new computer? No!

It is that associate's job to show you the next computer and then the next computer and then the next computer until you find what you are looking for OR YOU WALK AWAY.

The sales associate should NEVER be the one to stop the sale. That is your job as the customer.

Be The Sales Associate

When your shoppers come to your website it is ES-SENTIAL that you remember what your job is as the sales associate. Your job is to keep giving them options until they say "no" and/or "walk away". On your website this means they either stopped adding items to their cart and checked out or they left your website.

You should absolutely NEVER be the one to stop the sale.

How do you continue offering more products on a website? It's simple. In the product short description *(the text right next to the product photos)* you need to put sentences that say things like, "Click here for more dresses" or, "Shop bracelets here". Those sentences should be underlined and italic and, when clicked, take your customer to other products.

These links NEED to be "above the fold" *(the part of the page that is visible without scrolling)* because otherwise the Shopper may not see them. In fact, they most likely won't see them.

EVERY product on your website should have these links leading your Shoppers to the next product so that you are constantly offering them more. That's what it means to be a good sales associate and HELP your Shopper.

The links you provide on your Product Pages should make sense for the specific product. The easiest way to decide where to link the customer, is to think about the 2 types of Shoppers who may land on the Product Page. The Shopper will either love the product OR they won't.

If the product is a dress that the shopper doesn't like, it's likely they may be interested in other dresses. If the product is a dress that the shopper does like *(and is going to purchase)*, they may need a matching handbag or earrings or a sweater. Provide at least one link to direct the shopper to the next product.

By providing these links to coordinating or alternative products you are giving yourself one more chance to make a sale AND one more chance to raise the average order value with a Shopper who is already planning on making a purchase. It's a win-win because your Shopper gets a product *(or products)* they love and you make a sale.

Answer Their Questions

Another aspect of being a good sales associate is to know your products and be able to answer questions about them. Online it is important that these answers are quick and easy to find.

Depending on your product you need to provide different information. But, pretty much every single physical product should list the dimensions of the product, what it is made of, an explanation of how to use it, care instructions, how long until the product ships, and shipping cost *(especially if you offer FREE Shipping)*. Be sure that these questions are answered on EVERY Product Page.

If your product is one that typically results in additional questions be sure to answer those on every Product Page as well.

Show Them The Product

Your product photos are possibly the most important part of a Product Page. These photos need to provide enough information to convince someone to buy without ever holding the product in their hands. This can be hard to do.

It is incredibly important that each photo has a specific purpose and answers a very specific question. You should not have multiple photos that all have the same purpose.

It is a delicate balance between too many and too few photos. You don't want to cause "Analysis Paralysis" by giving too much information, but you also don't want to miss out on answering an important question and lose the sale.

For EVERY Product Page you need to have the following photos:
White Background Product Photo
(more info on these is in the chapter on Shop Pages)
Lifestyle Photo
(more info on these is in the chapter on Shop Pages)
Close-up Photo
(show texture/color/stitching/etc)
All product sides/angles
(show the back/front, inside/outside, etc)
Product size
(show this with a ruler or with a person)
Product packaging
(this shows the care you put into your product)

Go Above And Beyond

If you want to truly put your customer at ease and provide a connection to your brand, you'll also want to consider adding the following to your Product Pages:

Customer Reviews/Testimonials
(if you don't have reviews for the specific product use general reviews about your shipping time or how great you are to work with)

Product Videos
(help your Shoppers to REALLY visualize what it's like to have your product in their lives)

Social Media Links
(Shoppers who connect with your brand are even more likely to become raving fans)

Social Media Share Links
(the best way to get your customers to share is to ask them)

Email Sign-Up Link
(get the direct connection so that you can share even more with your Shoppers)

You Can Do It

If you've made it this far and started implementing these changes you are well on your way to improving the image you present to your customers and increasing your purchase conversion. Keep taking these steps to improve your website and before you know it you'll be ready to turn on the faucet of increased traffic to take your business to the next level!

CH 5 - OPT-INS

*It's Time to Sweeten
the Deal*

I used to work at Kohl's. One of my responsibilities was to change out the sale signage each week. I used to think it was hilarious that everything was always on sale. But, that was before I understood marketing.

Before you start to question my sanity...I want to explain that I am NOT suggesting that you should have sales on everything all the time. But, sales can be a powerful motivator.

I want to introduce you to Emily Smith. Emily is currently thinking about buying a new comforter set. She has found two different options & she likes them both equally. One is a little more expensive, though. Which one do you think she will pick?

So, you either suspected this was a trick & refused to answer, or you answered silently in your mind. Either way, I want to give you a few more details before you make your final decision.

The website that is offering the less expensive option *(let's call that comforter A)* is offering the product at the regular price. The website that is offering the more expensive option *(let's call that comforter B)* is offering the comforter at a discount of 20% off.

Even though Comforter B is on sale, it still more expensive than Comforter A. Now, which one do you think she will buy?

The easy answer seems to be that she'll buy the least expensive option *(sales shouldn't matter, right?)*. But, I hate to tell you that it isn't really that easy after all.

We all like to "win". There's something hard-wired into our brains that insists winning is best. If there wasn't,, we wouldn't have so many competitions, grades, and awards.

So, what does that have to do with sales? Well think about it, there's something about getting something on sale that makes you feel like you "beat the system". That you somehow "won" at shopping.

And that...that feeling right there...that's the thing that makes this "easy decision" so hard for Emily.

I mean after all, what if she gets Comforter A home and it turns out she doesn't like it? She may not be able to get Comforter B on sale later.

She starts to think a few extra dollars on Comforter B might make excellent sense after all. I mean she can always send it back and get Comforter A later if it turns out she doesn't like Comforter B & she won't miss out on anything because it's the regular price anyway.

I don't know what our fictitious friend Emily would

end up doing for sure. There are certainly times this logic makes me buy the higher priced item *(even though I know this tactic inside and out)*, but there are other times I buy the less expensive option. So, I can't say that this always works. But, I can say that once the customer gets the product in their house they are likely to keep it. So, you should do everything you can to get them to push that BUY NOW button.

The point of this little shopping excursion with Emily is to get you thinking. The fact is that you are competing with other websites with similar products RIGHT NOW.

What tools are you using to make sure they buy your product instead of someone else's?

Opt-Ins

Hopefully by this point, you have started making changes to your website to improve your Shopper's experience. Hopefully you have started overcoming objections & answering questions *(almost as if you were a psychic)*.

If you have, you are ready to start closing the gap between shopping and buying. The way to close that gap is with opt-ins.

What exactly is an "opt-in"? An opt-in requires the customer to give you something in exchange for something else. Typically, the customer is offering up their email address. What you are offering can vary greatly.

But, there are two main categories of opt-ins:
1. Purchase Incentive Opt-Ins
2. Non-Purcahse Incentive Opt-Ins

There are several ways to use opt-ins and I've mentioned several in this book already.

You should have an opt-in in your footer, on your homepage, and on every product.

You can also create special opt-ins to talk about on your social media & with your email list and then create special opt-in pages just for those.

Additionally, you should also have opt-ins in the form of pop-ups. But, be careful about having too many pop-ups because this can be a reason people leave your site.

I suggest having a generic exit intent/timed pop-up, plus a separate pop-up for exit intent in checkout.

You may also want to consider assigning a separate pop-up for your blog & other non-purchase pages.

Now, lets talk about a few types of opt-ins. Keep in mind, this is by no means an exhaustive list. Be creative & you can come up with many other types of opt-ins to grab your Shopper's interest.

Purchase Incentive Opt-Ins

Opt-ins with a purchase incentive are used to close a sale. These are the types of opt-ins that most of us think of in connection with ecommerce.

Here are some examples of purchase incentive opt-ins:
1. Percentage Off
2. Dollar Off
3. Buy 1 Get 1
4. Gift With Purchase
5. Free Shipping

Purchase incentives are great when used correctly. Before we discuss them further, I want to ask you a question...

Do you want to give a discount to someone who is going to buy even if they don't get a discount? Or do you only want to give a discount to close the sale with someone who may not have purchased otherwise?

I would like to suggest that if you give a discount to someone who would have purchased anyways, you are just giving YOUR money away for no reason.

There are some exceptions to this.

For example, I have an Etsy shop for my water bottle holders *(my shop name is Carry Clips, if you're interested)*.

I have a sale running on EVERY item in the shop at all times. This is because I know the power of a sale on a platform like Etsy. My product being on sale causes that same conundrum we discussed about Emily at the beginning of the chapter.

The difference is that my sale price is actually the price I want to make. In other words, I start with the sale price and add to it to get my "regular" price. So, I'm actually not losing anything by keeping it on "sale".

A second exception to the idea of not giving an incentive to someone who doesn't need it, is when you want to give a "gift" to your followers/fans/

previous customers. There can definitely be an argument made that these are EXACTLY the people you should be "rewarding" with discounts. After all, without them where would your shop be?

But aside from these exceptions, you shoudn't be giving away YOUR money for no reason.

I hope you agree with me, because I'm about to be controversial.

◆ ◆ ◆

Percentage Off

MOST shops I have offered my services to use a percentage off. MOST of the websites I've reviewed use a 15% or lower percentage.

In my opinion, 15% *(or less)* is not enough to convince someone to buy who wasn't going to buy already.

The feedback I always hear is, "But people use the coupon, so it's obviously working."

Let me ask you a question, "If you were going to buy something & I offered to give you 15% off on it, wouldn't you take the 15% savings?"

I'd bet your answer is, "Yes". I mean ANYONE would rather spend $85 than $100, right?

So of course some people are using it, if you're offering it.

My suggestion is to use a 20% off or larger incentive because this is enough to convince someone to buy who was hesitant. THOSE are the people you should be incentivizing to buy.

You want to get MORE sales, not the same number of sales and make less profit.

OK. So, that's my spiel about percentage off discounts. Feel free to disagree with me. But, I'd suggest testing it before you make any decisions. When I say test it, I mean get rid of the discount, see what happens. Bring back a 20% discount, see what happens. Compare everything.

Also, you can always raise your prices a little to compensate for the larger discount.

◆ ◆ ◆

Dollar Off

I actually prefer a dollar off incentive to a percentage off for most ecommerce shops because "money speaks".

Most people do not think in percentages. Most people do think in terms of dollars though.

The amount of the discount is going to have a lot to do with how expensive your products are. So, keep that in mind.

But, my suggestion is to never offer less than $10. Less than $10 isn't really enough to incentivize anyone to purchase.

You can always include a minimum purchase price if you need to keep a customer from trying to save $10 on a $10 item.

Here's an example of an excellent opt-in with a dollar off:

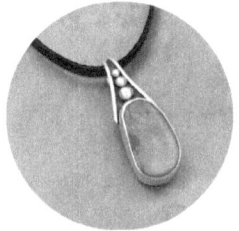

GET $10 TO SPEND

When you join the 10 Gables Gold Club today!

Email Address

First Name

SIGN ME UP

PHOTO COURTESY OF: 10GABLES.COM

Buy 1 Get 1

The next incentive is a Buy One Get One Free *(or 50% or some other iteration of this discount)*.
The advantage of this discount is that it is a good way to tell the customer what to buy. If you have an overabundance of an item, or if something isn't selling this can be a good way to start making sales on that product.

Gift With Purchase

A gift with purchase is an excellent incentive because you can use the ever-powerful word "FREE".

There's something about that word that can make people go crazy. We ALL love to get stuff for FREE.

That word has been the central theme of countless marketing campaigns and sometimes people will even wait in line for something FREE that they don't even really want.

So if you feel up to it, run a gift with purchase campaign and harness the word FREE.

Free Shipping

There's a reason that FREE Shipping is so popular on sites like Amazon, Etsy, & Ebay. It's because people hate being blind-sided with the cost of a product at checkout.

Offering FREE shipping can help prevent this cause of cart abandonment.

Here is an example of a FREE Shipping Incentive:

PHOTO COURTESY OF: MACHLAO.COM

◆ ◆ ◆

Non-Purchase Incentive Opt-Ins

Non-purchase incentive opt-ins are opt-ins that you can use without buying anything.

Here are some examples of non-purchase incentive opt-ins:
1. Giveaway Entry
2. Checklist
3. Tutorial

4. Screensaver
5. Phone Background
6. Printable

Why would you want to have non-purchase incentives? Because 98-99% of your shoppers *(on average)* are NOT making a purchase when they visit your website.

That means you NEED to get their contact information so that you can remind them that you exist and get them to come back and purchase later.

Giveaway Entry

A giveaway entry might be the perfect non-purchase incentive for your business IF:
1. You are not making your product OR if it is easy to make
2. Your products are not incredibly expensive
3. You are okay with spending a little money if it grows your email list

Here's an example of a giveaway opt-in:

PHOTO COURTESY OF: WWW.DEVILCLIP.COM

Checklist/Tutorial

There are several industries that lend themselves well to checklists & tutorials. Examples include anything connected to wedding, travel, or school.

So, if you find yourself in one of these industries OR you can think of a checklist/tutorial that lines up with your products, then offer your Shoppers some help. They'll love you for it.

Screensaver/Phone Background

If you are one of the small business owners who find themselves in an artistic field (*for example, drawing, or designing*), then this one is for you.

You can pretty easily take your designs/artwork and turn them into a digital version for your fans to use as screensavers or phone backgrounds.

And of course, even though it's free they have to provide you with their email address to get it.

BONUS: You can even turn this type of opt-in into a purchase incentive by offering the digital version when they buy the physical product.

Printable

Printables are also a great non-purchase incentive for the artistic among us. Create a printable greeting card or recipe card and offer that as a non-purchase incentive.

CH 6 - CHECKOUT

Closing the Sale

S usie Q needs to pick-up a few things at the store on the way home, but doesn't have much time. She stops anyway, hoping to get everything quickly. After gathering her products she heads to the cashier.

No one is at the register. She looks around and doesn't see anyone. Come to think about it, she's not sure she's seen anyone in the store at all.

Susie Q starts wandering around the aisles. 2 minutes pass. 5 minutes pass. Eventually she gives up, leaves her items on the counter, and walks out of the store.

Not only did she not get what she wanted, she wasted the very little time she had and now she doesn't have time to stop somewhere else.

Susie Q is NOT a "happy customer".

The same evening Jane Doe is also headed home and realizes she needs to grab a few things. She stops at a different store, runs through the aisles grabbing what she needs and heads to the register.

The cashier quickly checks her out and she is on her

way. Jane Doe is a "very happy customer".

When a Shopper visits your ecommerce store what is their checkout experience like? Do they leave your website a "happy customer"?

In this chapter we'll go through your checkout and touch base on a few issues that are common in ecommerce stores.

◆ ◆ ◆

Add To Cart

When a customer adds a product to their cart what happens? There are 3 ways to set-up your "Add to Cart" button.

The first option is for the customer to remain on the product page when they click "Add to Cart". This option may encourage your Shopper to keep shopping and adding more products to their cart, which is a great way to increase your average order value. But it means you are never actually asking the customer to complete checkout, which means you may suffer from increased cart abandonment.

The second option is for the customer to go to the cart when they click "Add to Cart". This option is great because it is moving them towards completing checkout so they are less likely to abandon the products in their cart. But it means that you may suffer from lower order values, because you are not encouraging customers to buy more products.

The third option is for the customer to remain on the product page, but have a popup that shows the current cart with a big "Checkout" button. This option is asking to close the sale, while also encouraging the customer to continue to shop.

So, which of the 3 options is the best? It really depends on what you are trying to do.

If you have trouble getting Shoppers to make a purchase, I'd suggest option 1.

If you have a good conversion rate and want to increase your average order value, you may want to experiment with option 2.

Option 3 is a good middle ground and it's great if you can set-up your website in this way. But, many web-builders do not have this as an option at all.

Now that you understand the options, the best course of action is to test them. Try using one option for a while and then switch to the other option and test again. Then you'll be able to compare your total sales and your average order values to get a clear picture of what is working best for you.

But, never forget that you can always change your "Add to Cart" action in the future, should your goals change.

◆ ◆ ◆

Cart & Checkout

You finally have your customer ready to place their order, but to keep them from abandoning those products in their cart you need to make sure you have a few important details in place to speed up their checkout.

First, you need to have a place for a discount code & preferably a pop-up to offer a discount if they try to leave your website. We'll talk a little more about pop-ups later, but suffice it to say that they are important *(even if they are annoying)*.

Second, it needs to be easy to remove products from the cart and get back to the products should they want to look at them again. This means there should be an easy "delete" button & the name of the product should be clickable. This is important because sometimes they start questioning which items they want to get and you want to make it easy to remind them exactly why they love each of them.

Third, your customer should be able to see the total cost of the products *(including shipping)* PRIOR to entering their personal information. If this is not possible with your platform *(it isn't for some)*, you should at least make sure to have the shipping cost spelled out in the cart, so they don't have to guess.

Fourth, you should offer a final opportunity to join your email list during checkout. But, be sure you include an incentive for the customer to join, otherwise they won't.

The final thing you want to make sure is present in your checkout is your logo. Hopefully, by implementing these other suggestions you will lower your cart abandonment. But on the chance someone does leave before completing checkout, you want to make sure they will recognize your brand. Recognition breeds trust and you want to make sure you start building that trust even if they do not make a purchase this time.

Remember the shoppers you read about at the beginning of the chapter? When you keep your checkout simple and easy to navigate, you will end up with your own "happy customers" who come back to buy again & again.

CH 7 - HOMEPAGE HELP

Attention, Information, & Next Steps

C ontrary to popular belief, your homepage is NOT the most important page on your website. But, it is still important and it is definitely important that it conveys the right information to your customers.

Just like every other page on your website, your homepage must do three things. First, it MUST capture your Shoppers attention. Second, it MUST inform the Shopper who you are. Third, it MUST tell the Shopper what to do next.

Unlike every other page on your website your homepage must continue to do these things OVER and OVER again in EACH section. That is what makes the homepage unique from other pages.

So, how do you capture your Shopper's attention, inform them who you are, and tell them what to do next on your homepage? You follow the "Section Formula".

Homepage Section Formula

EVERY section of your homepage should follow the Section Formula. The section formula is simple.

You need 3 things in each section of your homepage:
1. Title *(Each section title should use the SAME font, color, & text size)*
    The Title is responsible for grabbing the Shopper's attention
2. Content *(subtitle/image/video/text)*
    The Content is responsible for informing the Shopper about your brand/products/etc
3. Button *(Call To Action)*
    The CTA is responsible for directing your Shoppers to their next steps

PHOTO COURTESY OF: GATHERED-SOWN.COM

Let's explore how a section on the homepage uses the Section Formula to provide this info in the above example.

1. Title - Simple. Lovely. Leather. - Grabs the Shopper's Attention
2. Content - Image of the bag - Illustrates exactly what you sell
3. Button - Shop Now - Calls the Shopper to action

Here are a few more examples:

NEW! POTHOS COLLECTION

Pothos Desert Bloom Variscite Cuff
Sold out

Pothos Desert Bloom Variscite Ring
Sold out

Pothos Silver Pendant
$50.00

Pothos Silver Ring
$75.00

Pothos Silver Leaf Earrings
$40.00

VIEW ALL

PHOTOS COURTESY OF: 10GABLES.COM

The Go Lovely Promise

Adventurous souls need effortless jewelry with an artful touch. Forged in flame, our colorful, modern pieces help you escape the ordinary with jewelry as bold as you are. From workday to date or field to forest, each masterpiece moves your heart.

LEARN MORE

◆ ◆ ◆

Homepage Section Design

In addition to following the "Section Formula" each section of your homepage should be unique. It should be easy to immediately point out each section quickly *(without much effort or thought).* So your Shoppers can immediately find the information they are interested in.

One way to accomplish this is by separating each section by background COLORS to make identification of each topic easy for your Shoppers. When you combine this with Titles that are all formatted the same it makes it MUCH easier for your Shoppers to find answers to their questions quickly.

Every section of your homepage should also have a specific PURPOSE and answer a unique question. Do not use multiple sections that all have the same content/answer the same question in the Shopper's mind.

The sections of your homepage should each fit on ONE PAGE without scrolling. Your Shopper should be able to get the entire point without having to scroll back and forth.

Homepage Intro Section

Now that you understand how the homepage should be formatted, it's time to discuss the homepage content. The very first section of your homepage is the "Intro Section". The Intro Section is responsible for defining your brand.

The Intro Section of the homepage needs to provide the following information:
1. How the product helps them *(think about an emotional response or how it helps accomplish a goal)*
2. What the product actually is *(think of this as the product definition)*
3. An OBVIOUS call to action

PHOTO COURTESY OF: WWW.MYSCHEDULEDBIZ.COM

Let's explore how the Intro Section provides this information in the above example.

1. The product helps them move towards the goal of a successful business by helping the Shopper "Know Their Next Steps".

2. The product is "Targeted eCommerce Teaching".

3. The Call to Action is "Start Now". *(Most eCommerce Shops will use the CTA "Shop Now")*

You can see how with just these few lines of text and a button we are able to clearly define WHY the customer wants what we have to offer. That is what your Intro Section should be doing for your business.

Homepage Section Content

What belongs on the rest of your homepage? There are many options for content to include. But, EVERY ecommerce shop should include at least these 4 sections:

1. Shop Links

Take the Shopper directly to a specific product page when they click on it on the homepage

2. Testimonials/Reviews

Put the Shopper at ease & show that your shop is trust-worthy

3. Email Sign-Up

This should be in the actual content of the homepage not just in the footer & must have copy that makes the Shopper want to sign-up (review the chapter on Purchase Incentives for ideas)

4. Social Media Links

Direct your Shoppers to follow you on social media OR share your products on their social media

Once your homepage meets these standards you are one step closer to helping your Shoppers down the path to purchase by giving them the information they want in an easy to understand format.

APPENDIX I

Recommended Resources

One-On-One Business Help

Website Review Call - Make it easier for your customers to shop & ultimately buy your products
www.MyScheduledBiz.com/Easy

Google Analytics Review Call – Analyze where your traffic is coming from & which platforms create sales
www.MyScheduledBiz.com/Easy

Facebook Ads Manager Review Call – Grow your audience & understand how your ads perform
www.MyScheduledBiz.com/Easy

Homepage Usability Test - Focus your message & remove the barriers to purchase on your homepage
www.MyScheduledBiz.com/Easy

Small Business Tools

MSB Social – Schedule EVERY Social Media Platform, Understand Your Data, & Get More Sales
www.MSBsocialBlueprint.com

Storybrand – Find your "One Liner" & tell the RIGHT

story to your customer about your brand
www.youtube.com/watch?v=HFergIOUOAs

Hotjar - Watch how people interact with your page
https://www.hotjar.com/r/r5037b0 (Affiliate)

Acadium – Bring on interns to help with repeated tasks
https://app.acadium.com/r/3eljmdwj5 (Affiliate)

JustUno – Create Popups *(check w/website provider first; could also use Elementor, etc)*
https://www.justuno.com/

Zapier – Connect unrelated platforms *(Get notified in Slack/text message for every order)*
https://zapier.com/

IFTTT – Connect unrelated platforms *(Automatically repost social media to other platforms)*
https://ifttt.com/

Photo Editing Tutorial – WHITE background photos on Photoshop, Affinity Photo & Snapseed *(mobile)*
http://www.MyScheduledBiz.com/white

APPENDIX II

Photo Acknowledgements

Small Businesses Featured In This Book

Gathered & Sown - *Angie Gordon*
Handcrafted Leather Goods
www.Gathered-Sown.com

Machlao Studio - *Abby Winslow*
Vinyl Wall Decals As Unique As Your Faith
www.Machlao.com

Catch The Fire Worship Flags - *Andrea York*
Elevate Your Praise With Worship Flags
www.CatchTheFireWorshipFlags.com

10 Gables - *Christine Cravens*
Jewelry for Your Adventurous Soul
www.10Gables.com

I want to personally thank each of you for your continued support. I would not be publishing this book were it not for your love and prayers.

BROWSER vs BUYER

Optimize Your Ecommerce Website & Get More Sales!

Elise Nelson ■ MyScheduledBiz.com

ABOUT THE AUTHOR

Elise Nelson

Elise Nelson is the Founder & CEO of My Scheduled Biz, where she uses her 5+ years of experience as an ecommerce entrepreneur to help ecommerce shop owners increase their sales through website optimization.

With her straightforward, analytical style she brings clarity & answers the question burning in every entrepreneur's mind, "What should I do next?"

Elise lives outside Houston, Texas with her husband & daughter.

PRAISE FOR AUTHOR

Do you want a straightforward instructor who is sincere in her desire to help you? Then this is for you.

- BARB GRAJEK

3 orders in less than 24 hours. I was happy to get 3 orders in 3 months before. Before what?? Before making the changes to my website that Elise Nelson suggested! Coincidence?? I think not!! Elise you rock!!!!!

- RENEE WOODFORD

Elise makes my job as an entrepreneur SO MUCH EASIER. She is incredibly knowledgeable, always communicates and responds promptly, and she's great to work with. Thanks, Elise, for helping me be more successful without all the stress.

- ROSE MCCOMBS JORDAN